Rattler

by Mary Batten

Grosset & Dunlap
An Imprint of Penguin Random House

To my great-nephew Justin, who loves the outdoors—MB

GROSSET & DUNLAP
Penguin Young Readers Group
An Imprint of Penguin Random House LLC

Photo credits: front cover: Corbis/Joe McDonald; back cover: © Thinkstock/Fuse; page 1: © Thinkstock/johnaudrey; page 3: © Thinkstock/Don Stevenson; pages 4–5: © Thinkstock/PhilBilly; page 6: © Dave Bevan/naturepl.com; page 7: © Thinkstock/taburton; pages 8–9: © Thinkstock/SteveByland; pages 10–13: © Thinkstock/Fuse; page 14: (cactus) © Thinkstock/lirtlon, (snake) © Thinkstock/johnaudrey; page 15: © Thinkstock/GlobalIP; pages 16–17: © Corbis/Marc Rasmus; pages 18–19: © Corbis/Joe McDonald; page 20: © Thinkstock/de-kay; page 21: © Thinkstock/GlobalIP; pages 22–27: © John Cancalosi/naturepl.com; page 28: © Paul Berquist; page 29: © Thinkstock/twildlife; pages 30–31: © John Cancalosi/naturepl.com; page 32: © Thinkstock/johnaudrey.

Library of Congress Cataloging-in-Publication Data is available.

ISBN 9780448488417   10 9 8 7 6 5 4 3 2 1

At the end of a long, hot summer day, rattler crawls out of his hiding place. He is hungry. He has not eaten for two weeks. This isn't unusual for a rattlesnake. But now he needs to hunt.

Rattler waits for night to hunt.
Squeezing his long body into snaky curves, rattler slithers
along the ground. He moves quietly, smoothly, almost invisible
because his colors perfectly match the leaf litter and the dry grass.

Other night hunters also come out. A coyote howls. An owl hoots. Although rattler has no outer ears, he senses sound vibrations through his jawbones, which are connected to his inner ears. He probably hears only low-pitched sounds.

He can make his own sound with the rattle at the end of his tail, but he rarely uses it unless he is frightened by the sight of a coyote or one of his other enemies, like a skunk or a bobcat. The loud, hissy buzz of the rattle scares most animals away.

Rattler's eyes open wide to help him see in the dim light. Slithering along the ground, he moves his head from side to side. He flicks out his long forked tongue this way and that. He uses his tongue for smell, not for taste. By touching his tongue against a sensitive spot in the roof of his mouth, he can tell whether an odor is food, an enemy, or a mate. He comes to a burrow and sticks his tongue inside. But nothing is there. So rattler moves on. He has to find something to eat.

With special openings called pits behind each nostril, rattler senses the body heat of an animal coming closer. Food. The snake coils and waits. Closer. Closer. A mouse crawls along, looking for food. It doesn't see rattler until it is too late.

In a fraction of a second, rattler strikes, sinking his sharp fangs with their poisonous venom into the mouse's flesh. The fangs are hollow tubes that inject the venom like hypodermic needles. As soon as rattler bites the mouse, he lets go of the struggling prey. When rattler begins to close his mouth, his fangs swing backward. The mouse jumps into the air. But it cannot get away. Rattler stays still.

He waits for the venom to work. The mouse does not go far. The venom will kill it.

Rattler finds his dying prey by flicking his tongue to pick up the mouse's scent. When grabbing the mouse headfirst, rattler opens his flexible jaws wide so that his mouth becomes very large. Rattler does not chew his food. Instead he uses his neck muscles to swallow the mouse whole. Usually rattler hides while he digests his food, which may take several days, depending on the size of the prey.

After he eats, rattler will not need to hunt again for one to two weeks. He coils up to sleep when suddenly a family of skunks comes by.

The skunks, too, are hunting for food, and they do not see rattler. But they hear the hissy *BUZZZZZ* of his tail rattle. The skunks run away as fast as they can, but not before shooting off their smelly spray. Rattler hisses.

Each day is much the same for rattler. Since he is cold-blooded, he has to lie in the sun to warm his body. Then he hides and rests. When he gets hungry again, he hunts. There really isn't anything else for a rattler to do . . . until he needs a new skin.

Two or three times a year, rattler gets too big for his skin. When that happens, he sheds his old skin.

Rattler can tell when he needs to shed, because his eyes cloud over with liquid called mucus. The mucus is made by special glands in rattler's skin. The mucus helps to loosen the old skin, but it blinds rattler for several days. During this time, he stays hidden. Then he rubs his snout against something rough such as a rock or a shrub. First he loosens the skin along the edges of his lips. Scraping and rubbing, rattler crawls through his old skin so that it peels backward and turns inside out over the snake's body.

Shedding takes several hours. Getting the narrow neck skin over the thick middle of his body is the hardest part. Then rattler easily crawls through the remaining section, leaving the old skin in one piece, like a ghost rattler lying on the ground.

Rattler slithers away, looking like a new snake. The only sign of shedding is a new section in his rattle. The rattle is made of rings of keratin, the same substance that your fingernails are made of. Rattler makes his fearsome sound by shaking the rattle back and forth as fast as sixty or more times a second.

As the days get shorter and the air cools, rattler's body temperature drops. The environment controls his body temperature. In winter, he is very cold. The cold causes his heart to beat slower and his breathing to slow. To keep from freezing, he seeks shelter and joins other rattlesnakes in a den underground or in the rocks. There the snakes go into a deep sleep called *brumation*. For the next three to five months, they will not eat.

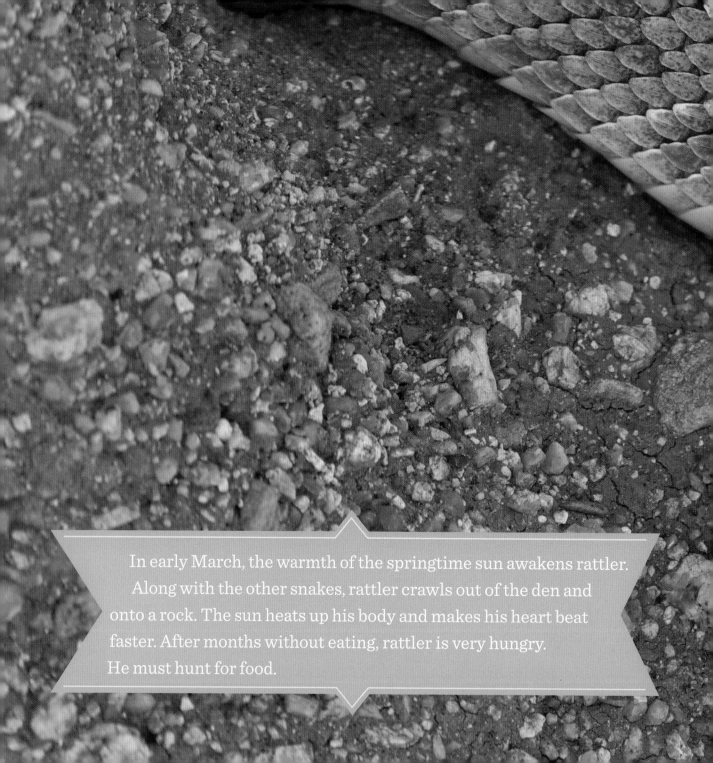

In early March, the warmth of the springtime sun awakens rattler. Along with the other snakes, rattler crawls out of the den and onto a rock. The sun heats up his body and makes his heart beat faster. After months without eating, rattler is very hungry. He must hunt for food.

His first meal is a ground squirrel—a big meal. During these first few weeks after brumation, rattler will eat a lot. He will also begin to look for a mate.

New leaves appear on the scrubby mountain trees.

Rattler's enemies begin stirring. Skunk and badger and bobcat are hunting.

Fox and hawk are hunting, too.

Everyone is looking for food and mates. Some animals are building nests and laying eggs. The mountains are alive with new life and new sounds.

Three months after mating, the female rattlesnake gives birth to eight to ten babies. The babies hatch from eggs inside the mother's body. They wriggle out into the world.

Baby rattlesnakes are born with a little rattle nub. They are also born with venom. Their bite can kill. From birth, the young ones have to hunt and survive on their own. But some mother rattlesnakes may stay with their babies about a week, until their first shed.

Few animals bother rattlesnakes. The hissy *BUZZZZZ* warns them to stay away. Rattler could live as long as twenty-five years doing his snaky things—slithering, hunting, sunning, sleeping, and shedding.